British Road Bridges – An Introduction

MARK CHATTERTON

First published in 2017 by Hadleigh Books as an ebook

This book is also available in the following formats:-

Mobi version for Amazon Kindle ISBN 978-1-910811-62-7
PDF file for Personal Computer ISBN 978-1-910811-64-1

www.hadleighbooks.co.uk

Front cover

The Clifton Suspension Bridge in Bristol, looking across the Avon Gorge from Clifton. Designed originally by Isambard Kingdom Brunel and Sarah Guppy, the bridge was first opened to pedestrians in 1864. Today, it still carries around four million vehicles a year over it, though there is a 20 mph speed limit, and heavy goods vehicles are banned from using it. The bridge is a grade I listed building.

CONTENTS

Introduction

As someone who has been visiting and photographing road bridges for several years, I have managed to glean plenty of information about this particular aspect of British engineering in my travels and research. It has been a fascinating journey, taking me from the far north of Scotland all the way down to Cornwall, with most of Great Britain in between. As no other books have been published on Britain's road bridges in this way to my knowledge, I have taken the liberty to write this short introductory book. It gives some basic information about the various types of road bridges that there are in Britain, the methods used to build them and the history behind some of these bridges. I will of course be publishing three longer books at a later date, which will go into greater detail about this interesting engineering phenomenon.

1 - DEFINITION OF A ROAD BRIDGE

For the purposes of this book, I would define a road bridge as a bridge which carries road traffic along its surface. In the majority of cases the bridge would be a crossing point over water, such as a river or a gap of water between the mainland and an island. In other cases, the bridge may transport road traffic across another road or a railway line, or an expanse of land such as marshland or scrubland.

Bridges are often classified according to their ability for bearing weight. The three main types of bridges are arch, beam and suspension, though of course there are variations of these three, as this book will describe. Some bridges discussed in this book may fall into more than one of these categories.

The main part of this book has been divided into two sections.

The first part looks at bridges that move or are moveable due to something needing the same space as the bridge. The second part is concerned with bridges that are fixed or stationary, and are not affected by another force needing the bridge to move.

For each type of bridge that I have covered, I have given examples of this type of bridge and have looked in detail at one of these examples, with a colour photograph of this bridge included with the text.

All the bridges discussed in this book go over water, though of course there are plenty of road bridges that go over other obstacles such as railway lines, other roadways and marshland.

2 - MOVEABLE BRIDGES

These can also be known as "Moving Bridges" and are bridges that move the roadway of the bridge so that some other form of transport - usually a boat - may pass through the same space.

In this section I have included the following types of road bridges:- Bascule Bridge, Swing Bridge, Transporter Bridge and Vertical Lift Bridge.

BASCULE BRIDGES

A Bascule Bridge is a moveable bridge which is able to come apart in order for boat traffic to pass along the waterway where the bridge previously was. Its name comes from the French word for "balance scale" and uses the principle of balancing a span whilst it is moved upwards to make room for a boat passing underneath it.

The most famous example of a Bascule Bridge is Tower Bridge in London where the roadway opens upwards to allow river traffic to pass under it. However, there are many more examples of this type of moving bridge which can be found in different parts of Great Britain. For example, the Corporation Bridge in Grimsby, Lincolnshire and the Walney Island Bridge, Barrow-in-Furness, Cumbria

TOWER BRIDGE, LONDON

One of the most iconic sites of London, Tower Bridge is the first bridge across the river Thames upstream of the sea, within the Greater London area. It was opened in 1894 by the then Prince of Wales, who later became King Edward VII. Construction had begun in 1888 and the bridge employed over four hundred workers, and cost over a million pounds to build.

The bridge needed to be a bascule bridge as many ships were still using the Pool of London, situated between London Bridge and the Tower of London. So, a public competition was held, with over fifty designs submitted. The bridge was designed by Sir John Wolfe Barry with Sir Horace Jones being the architect. The bridge had two bridge towers built on piers, with the central span being able to be opened and raised to allow ships to pass through the bridge. The two side spans of the bridge were actually suspension bridges.

Today the bridge is usually raised several times each week to allow shipping to pass through it. You can visit the bridge as a tourist attraction and walk along the upper walkways and look down onto the roadway and river below. The lower walkways were originally closed to the public in 1910 after gaining a reputation as a place where prostitutes and pickpockets frequented. The roadway is used by over 40,000 vehicles, cyclists and pedestrians each day.

ROLLING LIFT BRIDGES
See Bascule Bridge

SWING BRIDGES

A Swing Bridge is one where the bridge swings to the side either in one solid part or two separate parts, so that a boat may pass through the gap created. There are several examples of swing bridges in Britain, for example, the Crosskeys Bridge at Sutton Bridge in Lincolnshire, or the Whitby Swing Bridge in Whitby, North Yorkshire.

THE SWING BRIDGE, WHITBY

The Whitby Swing Bridge is a road bridge which goes over the River Esk in North Yorkshire. It was built in 1908-9 and designed by J Mitchell Moncrieff and replaced an earlier swing bridge which had been in place since 1833. It opens in two parts or "leaves" and is powered by electric motors. It originally carried the A171 through the town, but this was diverted in 1980 when a new high level bridge was built to the west of the town. It is only wide enough for one line of traffic, so traffic lights control the flow.

TRANSPORTER BRIDGES

A Transporter Bridge is one where a platform or "gondola" or "car", is suspended from the main bridge above by cables and transported from one side of the bridge to the other. There are just two working Transporter bridges left in Britain at the present time. These are the Tees Transporter Bridge in Middlesbrough in the North East of England and the Transporter Bridge in Newport, South Wales.

THE TEES TRANPSORTER BRIDGE, MIDDLESBROUGH

Sometimes known as the Middlesbrough Transporter Bridge or just "The Transporter", this bridge connects Middlesbrough on the south side of the River Tees with Port Clarence on the north side. It was opened in October 1911 by Prince Arthur of Connaught and replaced a ferry that previously operated here. The bridge is now a grade II listed building and the gondola is capable of carrying up to 200 people and 9 cars.

VERTICAL-LIFT BRIDGES

These are bridges where the roadway of the bridge is lifted vertically upwards above the water underneath it, so a boat may pass through unhindered by the bridge roadway. Examples of this type of bridge in Britain include the Kingsferry Bridge by the Isle of Sheppey in Kent, and the Centenary Bridge in Salford, Greater Manchester.

THE KINGSFERRY BRIDGE, KENT

The Kingsferry Bridge connects the Isle of Sheppey with the mainland to the north of Sittingbourne in Kent. It is a dual road and railway vertical-lift bridge which was opened in 1960, replacing two previous bridges on the site. The bridge can be raised to a maximum of 84 feet, when a klaxon is sounded to confirm the maximum height has been reached. It is powered by an electric motor underneath the road deck and there are two engine rooms on either side of the bridge which operate the lifting mechanism. It is made out of reinforced concrete.

3 – FIXED BRIDGES

These are also be known as "Stationary Bridges" and are bridges where the roadway is fixed into place, usually by pillars or cables. They are built high enough over the waterway so that boats can pass underneath them with plenty of space.

ARCH BRIDGES

These are bridges that use the shape of an arch to hold the bridge in place.

Although arch bridges were built as long ago by the Ancient Greeks, it was the Romans who first introduced arch bridges to Britain. The design was developed further in the Victorian age with the construction of railway bridges and eventually road bridges.

The load on the bridge can be pushed outwards and downwards due to its curved pattern. This force will vary in strength throughout the bridge and will be pushed towards the supports at either end.

The roadway can be situated above the arch, or beneath the arch or even in some cases going through the arch. The most famous example of this type of bridge in Britain is the Tyne Bridge in Newcastle-upon-Tyne. Other examples include the Runcorn Bridge over the River Mersey in Cheshire and the Grosvenor Bridge in Chester, Cheshire

THE TYNE BRIDGE, NEWCASTLE-UPON-TYNE

The Tyne Bridge has become one of the most defining symbols of the North East and was opened as long ago as 1928. It crosses the River Tyne between Gateshead to the south and Newcastle-upon-Tyne to the north. It is a through arch bridge, which means that the roadway goes through the arch rather than underneath or above it.

It was designed by Mott, Hay and Anderson, who also designed the larger Sydney Harbour Bridge in Australia, hence the similarities. The bridge itself was built by Dorman Long and Co. of Middlesbrough. The work on the bridge started in August 1925 and was completed in February 1928, with just one fatality, a scaffolder from South Shields. King George V and Queen Mary officially opened the bridge in October 1928.

The distinctive green colour of the bridge comes from the original green paint provided by J. Dampney and Co, of Gateshead. In 2000 the bridge was repainted using the same shade of green. The two towers are made from Cornish granite and were designed by Robert Burns Dick, a local architect. The towers did have lifts built into them as the bridge road deck is 83 feet (256 metres) above the river. These are now defunct. The bridge is 531 feet (162 metres) in length and is joined to the A167 (M) motorway at its northern end. It has the designated road number of the A167.

BEAM BRIDGES

A Beam Bridge is a basic bridge which spans two posts, towers or supports. The gap between the supports or abutments is known as the span. In basic terms a Beam Bridge is one where a slab of concrete or wood is placed over at least two abutments. Some Beam Bridges can be quite short, perhaps just a few hundred yards, whilst others can stretch for several miles. The downward forces on the bridge spread evenly all the way along the bridge, whilst the supports give an upward force which holds the bridge together. It can sometimes be known as a Girder or Box Girder Bridge. Examples of Beam bridges can be found throughout Great Britain, such as the Orwell Bridge over the River Orwell, near Ipswich in Suffolk; the Hildesheim Bridge over Weston-Super-mare railway station in Somerset; and the Tay Bridge over the river Tay near Dundee in Scotland.

THE TAY BRIDGE, DUNDEE, SCOTLAND

The Tay Bridge goes across the Tay Estuary in Eastern Scotland. It links Dundee in the north with Fife in the south and was opened in 1967. It is one of the longest road bridges in Britain with a length of 2250 metres and is an example of a Beam Bridge.

The Tay Bridge was designed by William A. Fairhurst and cost almost £5 million to construct. Work started in 1964 and took three years to complete.

There are forty two spans on the bridge with most of them being 55 metres in length, though there are four navigational channels which are 76.3 metres long. Until 2008 a toll was charged, but the Scottish government decided to scrap all tolls on its bridges in this year.

It has the designated road number of the A92 and is dual carriageway all the way across the river Tay. It saves vehicles from having to make a fifty mile detour via Perth to the west.

BOX GIRDER BRIDGES

This is where a bridge which has the main beams made up of girders in the form of a hollow box. It is basically a variation of the Beam Bridge, whereby the deck is built on or inside a hollow beam. In the Victorian era, Robert Stephenson used this design with the bridge he designed to carry the North Wales railway line across the river Conwy.

There are many examples of this type of bridge throughout Britain. Some of the main examples include: the Erskine Bridge near Glasgow, Scotland, and both London Bridge and Waterloo Bridge in London.

LONDON BRIDGE, LONDON

The current London Bridge was opened in 1973 after the previous version had been sold to American millionaire, Robert P. McCulloch for almost two and a half million dollars. It is an urban myth that he believed he was buying the nearby Tower Bridge. His version of London Bridge is now situated at Lake Havasu City in Arizona, USA. There have been at least four previous London Bridges in this vicinity going back to Roman Times.

The present London Bridge is a box girder bridge made from concrete and steel girders. It joins the district of Southwark and London Bridge railway station on the south bank with the City of London on the north bank.

It carries the A3 in five lanes over the River Thames and is 882.5 feet (269 metres) in length. The longest span on the bridge is 341 feet (104 metres) long. It was designed by the architect Lord Holford and was built by the contractors, John Mowlem and Co between 1967 and 1972 at a cost of £4 million. It was formally opened in March 1973 by Queen Elizabeth II.

CABLE STAYED BRIDGES

These are similar to suspension bridges in design, yet they are also similar to a cantilever bridge. They all have a tower or pylon which supports a deck below with several cables in tension. For shorter distances only one tower is needed to support the bridge. For longer spans, two or more towers may be used. There are many examples of this type of bridge in Britain including:- the Queen Elizabeth Bridge at Dartford in Kent, the Flintshire Bridge at Connah's Quay in North Wales and the Marine Way Bridge at Southport in Lancashire.

FLINTSHIRE BRIDGE, CONNAH'S QUAY, NORTH WALES

The Flintshire Bridge is a cable-stayed bridge which spans the river Dee joining Flint and Connah's Quay in North Wales in the south with the Wirral Peninsula in England to the north. It cost £55 million to construct and was opened in 1998 by Queen Elizabeth II.

It carries the A548 over the Dee Estuary and has been dubbed "the bridge to nowhere" by local people as it doesn't go on to any major city or road on either side of the river.

It is 965 feet (294 metres) long and the longest span on the bridge is 660 feet (200 metres). It was built between the years 1994 and 1997 by the Percy Thomas Partnership. Approximately 13,000 vehicles a day use the bridge.

CANTILEVER BRIDGES

This is where a structure sticks out from a support pillar in the form of a "Cantilever Arm", which is anchored at one end of the bridge, hence the name. The load is supported through diagonal bracing and they are really a modified form of the Beam Bridge. They usually have a truss formation in both the lower and upward parts of the bridge. The most famous example of this type of bridge in Britain is the Forth Railway Bridge in Scotland. However, there are several less "obvious" Cantilever Road Bridges in Britain, such as Wandsworth Bridge across the River Thames in London and the Battersea Bridge also in London.

WANDSWORTH BRIDGE, LONDON

The present Wandsworth Bridge was opened in 1940 during World War Two and was painted in a dull shade of blue to help camouflage it during air raids. Over eighty years later it still carries this same colour scheme. It replaced a previous bridge on this site which had been opened in 1873, though it was too narrow to carry buses and so a new bridge was recommended in 1926.

The present Wandsworth Bridge was designed by Sir Thomas Peirson Frank as a three-span cantilever bridge, wide enough to have two lanes of traffic in each direction.

It carries the A217 road between Parsons Green in Fulham in the north and Battersea/Wandsworth in the south. Over 50,000 vehicles a day use the bridge and it is 650 feet (200 metres) long.

DOUBLE DECK OR MULTI-LEVEL BRIDGES

This is when two levels of road or railway use the same bridge at different heights. This allows more traffic to be carried over a stretch of water in one go without the need for a second bridge. There are plenty of examples of this type of bridge throughout the world, though in Britain they are very rare. The best example is the High Level Bridge in Newcastle-upon-Tyne in the North East of England which carries both a railway and a road across the River Tyne in Newcastle-Upon-Tyne.

HIGH LEVEL BRIDGE, NEWCASTLE-UPON-TYNE

The bridge crosses the River Tyne between Newcastle and Gateshead with the railway track on the top and a roadway underneath this. It was opened in 1849 by Queen Victoria, having been built by the Hawks family from 5000 tons of iron. Local railway engineer, Robert Stephenson had designed the bridge which was built to join the railway network from the south up towards Scotland. Local motor traffic uses the roadway underneath the railway level, though this is now limited to buses and taxis due to weight restrictions. It has tied cast arches in its design and is now a Grade 1 listed building.

LATTICE BRIDGES

Lattice bridges use a variation on the design used in an arch, suspension or beam bridge. A lattice of steel girders is used in the sides and occasionally along the top of the bridge. Many railway bridges use this design, but there are very few road bridges like this. The two best examples are the Queen Alexandra Bridge in Sunderland and the Lady Bay Bridge, Nottingham.

THE LADY BAY BRIDGE, NOTTINGHAM

This bridge was originally a railway bridge carrying the Nottingham to Melton Mowbray railway across the River Trent in Nottingham. It closed to railway traffic in the 1960s, but it was another twenty years before the bridge was opened to road traffic.

It now connects Meadow Lane on the north bank with Radcliff Road on the south bank.

SUPSENDED SPAN BRIDGES

- see Cantilever Bridge

SUPSENSION BRIDGES

This is when the roadway or deck is hung by cables from a supporting pillar. Cables fastened to the ground at each end of the bridge are used to secure the bridge. The cables then cross over a tower near to the ends of the bridge. The road deck is then supported by suspender cables which are joined to the main cables.

In the early days of suspension bridges, rope was used for the cables. Then in Victorian times iron chains were used, such as in the bridges designed by Thomas Telford. Finally in the twentieth century steel cable was used. The cables have the effect of supporting the weight of the deck and the load on it.

There are several types of this bridge in Britain, including the Tamar Bridge, linking Plymouth in Devon with Saltash in Cornwall;, the Forth Road Bridge at Queensferry in Scotland; and the Humber Bridge near Hull linking East Yorkshire with North Lincolnshire.

THE HUMBER BRIDGE

When it was first opened to road traffic in 1981, the Humber Bridge was the longest single-span suspension bridge in the world, with its 7,280 feet (2,220 metre) length. It held this record until 1998 when the Akashi Kaikyo Bridge was opened in Japan.

It is called the Humber Bridge as it spans the Humber, an estuary formed by the confluence of the rivers Trent, and Ouse. It joins Hessle on the north bank with Barton-on-Humber on the south bank.

An idea for a bridge across the Humber was mooted as far back as the 1920s, but it wasn't until the 1960s that the government of the day sanctioned the building of the bridge and work finally started in 1972.

The bridge was formally opened by Queen Elizabeth II in July 1981, after having been opened to traffic in June 1981. The bridge is now connected to the motorway network of the M62 on the north side and the M180 on the south side, saving fifty miles off the original journey between Hull and Grimsby.

THROUGH ARCH BRIDGES

A Through Arch Bridge is a bridge built in the traditional arch shape which has the roadway placed somewhere through it. Examples are the Tyne Bridge in Newcastle-upon-Tyne and the Silver Jubilee Bridge in Runcorn, Cheshire.

SILVER JUBILEE BRIDGE, RUNCORN, CHESHIRE

Also known for many years as the Runcorn Bridge, the Silver Jubilee Bridge joins the towns of Runcorn and Widnes across the River Mersey. It was opened in 1961 as a replacement to the previous Transporter bridge across the River Mersey.

It has a main arch span of 361 yards (33 metres) and was widened in the mid-1970s. It has been replaced as the main crossing over the River Mersey in this vicinity with a new bridge called the Mersey Gateway. The Liverpool to London railway line runs next to the road bridge on the far side of this photograph.

TIED ARCH BRIDGES

These are sometimes called a Bowstring Arch or a Bowstring-Girder Bridge and are variations of the basic arch bridge format.

The arch part of the bridge is tied to the roadway by a series of cables vertically placed all along the bridge.

Examples of this type of bridge are the City Bridge over the River Usk at Newport in South Wales; the Bonar Bridge on the old A9 in North East Scotland; and the Wearmouth Bridge over the river Wear in Sunderland.

THE WEARMOUTH BRIDGE, SUNDERLAND

The Wearmouth Bridge in Sunderland is the first bridge over the River Wear nearest to the North Sea. It was opened in October 1929 by the then Duke of York, before he became King George VI. The 1929 bridge replaced an earlier bridge which had stood on the site since 1796, though it was reconstructed by Robert Stephenson in 1859.

It was designed by the firm of Mott, Hay and Anderson, who also designed the nearby Tyne Bridge and the Sydney Harbour Bridge. It was built by Sir William Arrol and Company Ltd, based in Glasgow, who also built the Forth Rail Bridge and Tower Bridge in London.

It is both a tied arch and through arch bridge with a span of 375 feet (114 metres). It connects the city centre of Sunderland in the south with the district of Monkwearmouth to the north and carries the A183 merged with the A1018 across it. When it was first opened, trams as well as motor vehicles used the bridge. Trams stopped using the bridge in 1954. The bridge is Grade II listed.

TRUSS BRIDGES

A Truss Bridge is one where straight beams in the form of triangles are used in the construction. This makes the best use of the strength which is found in the triangle shape. These transfer the load on the deck into the piers and usually consist of several triangular sections welded together to form the bridge.

This sort of design is more popular in railway bridges as they are capable of carrying heavy loads not usually found in normal road traffic. However, there are some road bridges which are Truss Bridges. The best example in Britain is the Queen Alexandra Bridge crossing the river Wear in Sunderland.

THE QUEEN ALEXANDRA BRIDGE, SUNDERLAND

Originally the Queen Alexandra Bridge was both a road and railway bridge on two levels, with the railway deck above the roadway. Due to a decline in railway traffic using the bridge in the early twentieth century, the railway level of the bridge was closed in 1921. The bridge had been opened in 1909 by the Earl of Durham and was designed by Charles A. Harrison as a steel truss bridge.

However, the bridge is still used by large amounts of motor traffic going across the river Wear between the Deptford and the Southwick areas of Sunderland. On the north side you can still see the remains of the original railway bridge which was cut away from the main bridge in the 1920s.

4 - USEFUL WEBSITES

Here are some websites which are connected in some way with road bridges. Please note that the author and Hadleigh Books cannot be held responsible for the content and functionality of these websites.

Roads & Bridges – An American online magazine which covers the construction side of roads and bridges mainly in the US. https://www.roadsbridges.com/

The Forth Bridges website – Website which covers all three bridge crossings between Queensferry and Dalmeny in Scotland. https://www.theforthbridges.org/

The Tay Road Bridge website – Information on the Tay Road Bridge.
http://www.tayroadbridge.co.uk/

Tower Bridge website – Information on the history of and visiting information for Tower Bridge in London.
www.towerbridge.org

Sabre – The Society for All British and Irish Road Enthusiasts. The website has a huge section on the road bridges found in Great Britain and Northern Ireland.
www.sabre-roads.org.uk

ABOUT THE AUTHOR

One of the first bridge crossings that the author Mark Chatterton made was crossing the River Mersey between Widnes and Runcorn on the newly opened Runcorn Bridge in the early 1960s. This superseded the old Transporter Bridge between the two towns and was a vast improvement. Now fifty years on the suspension bridge is once again being superseded by a newer bridge between Widnes and Runcorn, called The Mersey Gateway. Mark has written extensively on the British transport infrastructure for several years now. For this book Mark has travelled all over Great Britain researching and photographing Britain's road bridges. This is the first of four books on Britain's road bridges by Mark.

www.markchatterton.com

OTHER TRANSPORT BOOKS

BY MARK CHATTERTON

On the following pages can be found a selection of British road based transport books by Mark Chatterton.

They can be bought from most bookshops or online at:- www.hadleighbooks.co.uk

BRITISH MOTORWAYS –

AN INTRODUCTION

British Motorways - An Introduction gives the reader a glimpse into the world of motorways in Britain. It looks at famous motorways like the M1, the M6 and the M25, as well as giving details of the longest, widest, shortest and busiest motorways. There are over twenty colour photographs included in the book and also a list of all the motorways in Britain.

Printed book ISBN: 97810811610
E Book ISBN: 97810811603

Published by Hadleigh Books

BRITISH ROAD TUNNELS –

AN INTRODUCTION

British Road Tunnels - An Introduction looks at the various types of tunnels that are found in Britain, as well as the different methods of constructing them. Included are over twenty colour photos and background information on each included tunnel.

Printed book ISBN: 97810811573
E Book ISBN: 97810811566

Published by Hadleigh Books

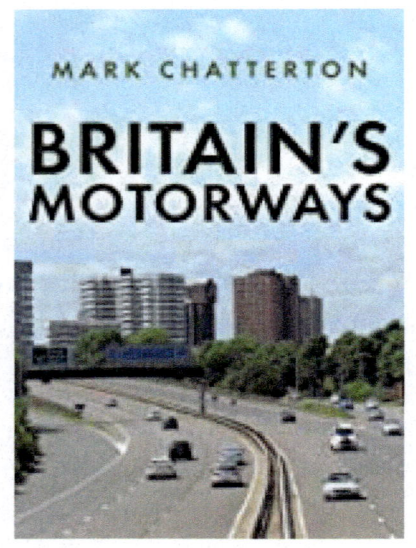

BRITAIN'S MOTORWAYS

This is a more detailed book than *British Motorways - an Introduction.* It looks at every motorway there is in Britain from the M9 and M90 in Scotland right down to the M20 in Kent and the M5 in Devon. It contains detailed entries of almost seventy motorways, as well as over a hundred colour photographs with detailed information on each motorway. There are many other facts and figures about Britain's motorways included including motorways in films, on TV, smart motorways, events which have closed motorways and motorways service stations.

Printed book ISBN: 978139811165
E Book ISBN: 978139811172

Published by Amberley Books

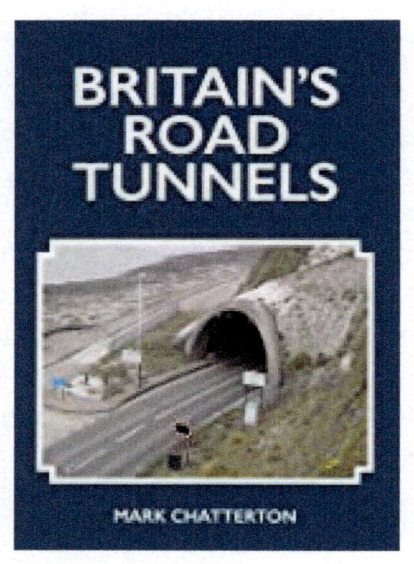

**BRITAIN'S
ROAD
TUNNELS**

MARK CHATTERTON

BRITAIN'S ROAD TUNNELS

This is a more detailed book than *British Road Tunnels – An Introduction*. It looks at every road tunnel to be found in Great Britain whether it be on a motorway, an A-road or in a small street. There are chapters on road tunnels at airports, railway stations and shopping centres. Famous tunnels discussed in the book include the Blackwall Tunnels, the Dartford Tunnels, the Mersey Tunnels and the Hindhead Tunnel. There are approximately 100 colour photographs included as well as a links page.

Printed book ISBN: 9781398100282
E Book ISBN: 9781398100299

Published by Amberley Books

Printed in Great Britain
by Amazon

83561808R00047